VA

# VANISHING ACT

# ACT

## GILES BLUNT

Library and Archives Canada Cataloguing in Publication

Blunt, Giles, author
Vanishing act / Giles Blunt.

Poems.
Issued in print and electronic formats.
ISBN 978-1-55096-583-4 (paperback).--ISBN 978-1-55096-586-5 (pdf).--
ISBN 978-1-55096-584-1 (epub).--ISBN 978-1-55096-585-8 (mobi)

I. Title.

PS8553.L867V35 2016          C811'.54          C2015-908659-0
                                               C2015-908660-4

Second Printing, 2018.
Copyright © Giles Blunt, 2016
Design and composition by Mishi Uroborus;
typeset in Fairfield, Bembo and Trajan fonts at the Moons of Jupiter Studios.
Cover image "Glowing Lines" by Daan Roosegaarde and Heijmans Infrastructure.

Published by Exile Editions Ltd ~ www.ExileEditions.com
144483 Southgate Road 14 – GD, Holstein, Ontario, N0G 2A0

Some of these poems were printed previously in *Exile: The Literary Quarterly*, *Grain*,
*Stardancer*, *Nebula*, and *Poetry Canada Review*. Excerpts from "Vanishing Act" appeared in
*The Arvon Anthology of Poetry*, edited by Ted Hughes, Philip Larkin, and Seamus Heaney.
*Three by Lauren* appeared in Giles Blunt's novel *The Hesitation Cut*, published by
Penguin Random House Canada.

We gratefully acknowledge the Canada Council for the Arts, the Government of Canada
through the Canada Book Fund (CBF), the Ontario Arts Council, and the Ontario
Media Development Corporation, for their support toward our publishing activities.

Canadian Sales: The Canadian Manda Group, 664 Annette Street,
Toronto ON  M6S 2C8    www.mandagroup.com    416 516 0911

North American and International Distribution, and U.S. Sales:
Independent Publishers Group, 814 North Franklin Street,
Chicago IL 60610  www.ipgbook.com  toll free: 1 800 888 4741

*To Peter Dubey*
*and*
*Donald Lorimer,*
*who couldn't stay*

*contents*

# WHO I WASN'T | 11

# THREE BY LAUREN | 29

# VANISHING ACT | 37

# WHO I WASN'T

# Lazarus

## I

One lifetime was enough; I bore my days
As well as any fool, chewed my portion
Of decay, nourishing a quiet scream.
Look at Lazarus, they sighed, what a man,
In bald old Bethany not one sinner
So equable, serene, so meek of eye.

It's true I was mindful of my blessings:
There was a bright day in Jerusalem,
The gold light falling, a fine gust lifting,
I perched like a buzzard on the wall
Gazing at the marketplace, the beggars,
The blind, their harmonious diseases
—O Israel, perhaps I did not love
But I felt emptied that day of hatred
Such gold the sun scattered at their black feet!

Remember your epiphanies, oh yes:
In half-light of a summer dusk as leaves
Hung down fatigued, hour and sky were folding
On the hill just west of town, a quiet fire.
I sat on the swing I made as a child
So crooked and uncomfortable it creaked

Beneath my weight. And lobbing to and fro,
Suspended, kicking gently back and forth,
A normal man with rope and bits of wood
In pointless motion inches from the earth,
I realized the miracle of flight.
I watched the sad-eyed children walking home
I heard their little skeletons click by
Pointing at me in the failing light
A skinny human hanging from his tree.

In truth, they make me sick, the villagers
So sick I nearly packed it in again
But there's no rush—one deathbed was enough.
I've lost my old concern about perfection
Perfection is death, perfect men are dead
And in this climate gods do not last long.
I think I knew one, we killed him quickly
Earth must be the Bethany of heaven.
Three dying men were slung up on the hill,
A belt of stars around the afternoon.
Their broken bodies twinkled, slick with rain.
Earth must be the Golgotha of heaven.

## II

A need for closing everybody's eyes
I always had a need to disappear
Not surprising Lazarus died so young
And coming back all those damned emotions
Coming back to him to her to me we
Huddled naked in the room the dim light
All the lovers cursing one another
I was one I tried to cry and could not
Among such quantities of flesh and hair
The dim light just sufficient to perceive
The eyes the teeth and nothing to describe
The blank walls and the bodies of the three
I was one wanting to cry and not being able
And she wanting to touch and not being able
And he not caring to be touched at all
The atmosphere so chill it made him shy
So loud the curses and the cracking sound
When all the pretty bridges split apart
The delicate constructions of our youth
All splintered up nothing left but curses
Wanting to speak and not being able
Gazing at the bits of bridge the ruin
None of us could resurrect none able
Not a syllable yet all mouths open
Coming back a lot of noise coming back
The summing up and then the coming back

The sleeping yes the quiet and the death
I could have used before the summing up
What could I say I tried to love mankind
But could not do it tried to love the wife
But lacked the strength or will pretended
Far too long to continue to pretend
Mistook relief for something else again
I have slept with thirty women I said
I had three friends and never liked children
I often drank beyond obliteration
Paralysis helped me love my neighbour
Moses did I ever love my neighbour
All the strangers kissing in the gloom
The dim light just sufficient one could kiss
Whatever was at hand to plug the holes
I swear I kissed a thousand strangers
To keep the inside in the outside out
It's a common story not all that bad
Nothing you could drop a man in hell for.

# After the Photograph

What you have chosen I have chosen
To abandon. Your steps in the distance
Mine in the present, will be soundless
Unceasing, in London and forever
Dying and alive. That final day.

Beyond the veil of rain
A seagull circled upward out of sight
Climbing into sound approaching voice
The rain, the lake
The outline of a hill
Encountered
And arranged themselves
According to that voice.

Such magic was the magic
You were born for
But you demanded darkness
You said I'm hungry for the night
Still
That seagull rides forever out of sight
That blotch of soaking pine remains the hill.

On what domain, what range
For and according to what?
It never mattered, never will
Your eyes are red and fixed upon
The jagged end of life, which lends us
Every good and perfect gift.

This clinging sorrow cloaks a disowned beauty
Yet the cloak becomes in this way beautiful
I remember how you looked that night
Foreign and more foreign, yes
And close my eyes to listen for
Your soundless, your unceasing steps.

# December, Queen Street

The lovers in their hoods
Had kiss upon kiss

So many kisses
Yet no two the same

A drunk man drooled
Until the streetcar came

And snowflakes twirled
No two the same

Bits of a universe
Whiter than this

# Night in the Gatineaux

Lights on a long bridge undulate and flicker
Dipping just so, yellow pinpricks beckoning
One who swims out, looks to the bridge and stretches
      Aching to rest there

Black and dead winds hover at the riverbank
Silence the water and the weaving branches.
Yet that swimmer crawls in his windmill motion
      Caught in a nightmare

Patiently one waits, elbows on the bridge rail,
Idly sings an ancient song of widowhood.
Night is her black shawl, wreathes of night the only
      Flowers you give her

Clusters of stars are pinned to the Gatineaux
(One will ignore them; one marks how they gather)
Thus dividing, ever, one on the bridge from
      One in the river

Question: what girl, night, or song in a female
Throat shall hang you up in that collection?
See the shoreline vanish, even as water
      Drips from your finger

# The Obscure Lover

Very well, she stamps her foot.
How am I to guess
Attacked with such dumb rage
What fears pour down from either fist
I know
By the scars on each thin wrist
That love is glass between our lips
And therefore I remain
A storm distilled upon a windowpane.

Tears again.
Old flames flutter on her brow
And rising up like smoke
A crowd of men
Obscure the lover calling from the bed
Rage, wrist, fist and flame are blurred
Across the image of her choice
Who hangs a silence over every word
And knots a ribbon round her voice.

She turns a touch into a fight
She turns away
But I have seen those shoulders when
The yellow light
Clung like sweat to her fine skin

She stretched by the window
Loose-limbed and warm
Her reflection wrapped around the August night.
Very well, turn away,
And I will be silent now as then.

# Three-by-Five

Boys call
Along the shore
For you. They do not hear
Your silk voice rising from the lake,
My name.


She said:
I am a verb
Love is a syllable
Say but the word and my spirit
Is healed.


Cars crawled
Six floors below
Through slush. Nearly an hour
She stood with her brush in her hand
Watching.

# The Renunciation

*"As if there were any difference between perishing and being another thing!"* —ERASMUS

### I

Light from a streetlamp quivers in your tears
You are afraid, you say, to recognize
The facts. The snowflakes fall, the night creeps by
And still you lean lamenting all the love
You must forsake. Take a look around.

You thought some wary angel treads a path
Before your feet, distinguishing the right,
The wrong, the best, the worst, from all the sweet
Temptations luring you. No doubt
Dilemmas break like glass before his wings,
His hair a golden tent in bitter fields,
Celestial philosophies his gift,
Angelic fingers, ministering hands
Caress you when your heart leaps into flame.

You thought this was religion beckoning
With oh such knowing eyes, such ancient robes,
A breathless flock falls on its knees before
The wizard turning wisdom into wine.
They'd hear a sin or two without reproach

Forgiving all you dare to let them know
Confessions turn to sermons at your touch—
In autumn, consolations from the leaves,
A crocus and a crucifix in spring
In summer, allegories of the lake
And swaddling flesh in winter anecdotes
Would be your blinding gift.

Anoint yourself.


II

The streets fan out like spokes from where I stand
Remembering the window where your face
Your face expressionless, not quite serene
Without the chance of words, without a voice
Hovered for a moment then receded
To leave the empty glass, my empty face.
–Surrender every future to your past
Betray your sleeping heart and let it sleep.

They tell me I am young, the future's mine
Come peace or war but no, I disagree.
For some, there is no war but only winter.
I do renounce that hopeful face that grins
From nineteen fifty-five; I do renounce

That string of ghosts and hang them out to die
Not me—no, no, not me—they never were.
These days I keep the planet to myself
When words like dreams and feathers fall away.

Now if it die, the earth or what remains
Shall spin its ruined wisdom round to some
Disinterested king. Some idle Zeus,
Remembering a vaguely bluer world sweeps up
The dust of his disintegrated angels
The sullen children gathered there await
His soft command, his benedictive smile
Incorporating rock among the jewels
This widowed world in benedictive grace.

# THREE BY LAUREN

# Darling

Darling, when you come
Inside me, then you go away
It's okay, it's okay

I've no idea what you're after
Take whatever you need
I won't bleed, I won't bleed

You are smoke and lightning
I am ashes, skin, and hair
I don't care, I don't care

Forget my name, it's written where
So many dead girls signed
I don't mind, I don't mind

Sink your teeth into my throat
Come in my face, come in my hand
I understand, I understand

But darling, when you come
Inside me, I can see my breath
Love is colder than death
Love is colder than death

—LW

# Thin Ice

You loved me on skates
My taste for sharp objects
Pirouettes, figure eights
I knew you liked watching
You knew my feet bled

Only once I fell
My smile never slipped
The crowd never guessed
I have a hot red wound
A hot glass heart
For girls
Well and truly doomed
Love is the transparent art
For certain girls
Thin ice is best

I was your daughter
You taught me how to bleed
If summer comes
I'll skate on water
But for now you can read
My crimson
Hieroglyphics

I'll skate away
Let me break
Let me make
Something ragged, something raw
Something difficult to take

I swear by the blades
Beneath my feet
Part of me
Wants to kill me
That's the part
I want to meet.

          —LW

# Leg-hold Trap

*Hold* is a kind word for it
As if he said caress
When what he meant was
I'm going to break your leg
Into a red unholy mess

No need to shriek
No need to beg
He's only *holding* your leg
This isn't hell you're in
He doesn't hate you, after all
He only wants your skin

You have a choice
You have teeth
You know exactly what to do
Just chew your way
Through bone and sinew
Tendons, veins, and nerves

No one's forcing you to stay
Run away
Run away

—LW

# VANISHING ACT

# The Car

I T WAS DAWN when a long beach hove into view. I nosed the car into an access road curving down toward the sea.

The car had been travelling at high speed when I came to behind the wheel. That would have been near midnight; I had been unconscious for some time. Lit by a red moon rocks hills and forest had bounded out from obscurity toward the car tumbling into sure oblivion behind.

An army of young mothers lay stretched along the beach their bellies empty of infants. The babies it seemed had departed and fathers sat in groups muttering to each other.

A wooden dock and on the dock a child—the only child in this particular bay of creation. He wielded a hammer and was using it to nail a sunfish to the dock.

# Fool

The fool was waiting for the light to change
He staggered at the curb    half crippled
by the fortune on his back    a frail sack
of needs and souvenirs. Blond hair
flicked across his face    memories beyond
recall propelled him here and there:

A chase through rain and thunder
cunt borne down on the wet savannah
eyes in the cave the cave itself
the blood the birth the god the flood
had brought him to this pass

The far sun rose
on mountain peaks where mathematicians lift
and swing their symbols glittering with snow
In pairs they calculate the beauty
of a fool about to die
the lowest common hunger
meekest common cry

And there he stood
a young man three parts wishes one part dreams
and yearned for women     women linked
their arms around him in a chain
The Virgin Mother and the Whore
came down on summer nights
and lured him to a ruin
where he wept.

But those hooded mathematicians!
That book with its crust of snow!

# Pick a Card

I STOPPED AT THE HIGHWAY trying to decide whether to turn back or move on. Either way the car exuded confidence, which was no help at all.

A glance in the rear-view mirror. The sea like glass. Sail of a departing ship. I turned to look. Nothing but flat grey sea. A creative vehicle, this car.

I shoved it in gear and headed for home.

# Host

You rode the subway to the garden gate
Beyond the wall a crowd of guests
absorbed you in a ring
So like your own the pairs of moving lips
and the host just a rumour among them
The pairs of abstracted intelligent eyes
the delicate ears     so like your own
the thudding feet. The ruddy faces
when the host appeared turned blank.

The host was a young man
sleek and strange
a young man practiced in the art of change.
He plucked a dream from behind your ear
and flung a group of figures on the wall
figures from a dream beyond recall:

About a deathbed family members kneel
in love and hate     kneel down
confess in rage confess too late.
Their words turn into silver as they fall
—nickels dimes and quarters in a heap.

The tree went black with crows.
The wall had crumbled
the guests gone.
Above the sound of breaking laws
nothing can be heard
the crows turn pale
and at your feet
the snake that was his belt
devours its tail

# Lucy

L UCY WAS COUCHED in the back of my thoughts as if upon a rumble seat. Was she behind this mobile opulence? Lucy had a degree in physics and a hungry mouth but her power was most keen when her whereabouts was unknown.

Clouds purple and black. Winter biding its time above the hills. I had the landscape and the highway to myself—almost. I had to overtake the odd truck. But nothing passed me unless it was travelling the other way and thus irrelevant.

I had reason to believe Lucy was living in Virginia with the previous case but this was by no means certain.

# Priestess

I who dangled starving from your breast
Come back because I heard you call
A fragrant summons on the purple light
Or thought I heard—do you forget?
Tonight I can remember all.
Mine was the curse of a virgin birth    remember?
The babe purloined?
The babe you dipped in flame?
He wants his name

Eve before Adam
You wandered through the wood
With clear untroubled eyes
And men died    men died
Among your suitors hanging one by one
Their bodies twisting    creaking in the wind
You set your temple and began your book
A History of the Soul.

Oh Lady of the Delta hear
The rain tick down beyond your throne
Where palms and pomegranates weave
You sit between the pillars    black and white
Your womb degrading slowly into stone

The mandolins are winking     chanting over there
I must go by     I will ignore
Your shoulders hard as flint
The lap of stone where young men weep
But I will keep
Your love no deeper than a fingerprint
Your History of the Soul

# Marriage

HAZE BROODED OVER a maze of suburbs. I turned my attention to the interior. Smells of leather and new carpet. I tried the radio. The numbers throbbed but it said nothing. Between stations. I flipped each switch, pushed every button. Lights wipers vents all in working order. I switched everything off except the radio. I adjusted the seat and settled into folds of red leather. I would never leave this car.

A city rose from the horizon brick by brick.

# River

I still see her face     so young so fine
The feline smile as if she held the taste
Of summer's day dissolving on her tongue.

I see the wheatfield rippling in the sun
The grove of chittering cypress trees
That field where she unfolded like a hand

A god will hunt you down she said move on
Between the cypress trees a river runs
A strand of thought, a theory to the sea

And still she holds me in the flagrant sun
The yellow wheat, my best hallucination
Realest home.

# Asleep at the Wheel

A CASE OF highway fatigue was setting in. Fortunately the car answered easily to the slightest suggestion. I let the road unreel before me at cruising speed while I considered Lucy. The causes and effects.

Day after day alone in the apartment I had found myself up against the mirror. It wasn't vanity. I wasn't searching for points of interest or signs of aging. Often my legs would begin to ache from standing so long in one position. I would move away. Stare out the window. Pace the hall. Only to creep back to the mirror. Humiliated.

After Lucy had come and gone I recognized this as a symptom of unrequited love for no one.

The night I met her—it was at a party—she pressed a scrap of paper into my hand. Her phone number. Later as I waited for a bus in the sub-zero cold I knew I would go out of control and wondered when I'd ever been in control.

What movie is this? she said when I knelt to kiss her knees.

# King

Old king when you abandoned me to drown
When the capsized boat and the tiny keel
Drifted down to a freckle in your eye
Did you bear like a soldier this heart-felt loss?
What word of hope what likely tale
Did you spin for your wretched queen?

Your guard turned me away
—My hair was wild my costume strange—
And so I come disguised
I come back ugly and unshod
Bearing for proof the brand you seared
Into my flesh a jealous god

Translation has disfigured the original
Left me somewhat altered
Your baby's skin was soft
Your baby's breath was sweet
Bend down your grizzled head come kiss
The grey shape looming at your feet

But keep your throne

All is stable here old ruler
The wind is fresh and the light clear
A balance of palette and sword
Brings peace where the orchards bloom

I do not want your throne but you remember:
When your royal arm grows thin
And weak and cannot lift a spoon
A debt is cancelled and a fortune paid

My little boat is bobbing at the shore
Step with me down the curving stair
Again to that wide river
And if I lean well forward with the oar
You who cannot love me shove me
Off to finer kingdoms like a prayer

# Lucy's View

THE EXPRESSWAY was overhung with lights that shed a butterscotch glaze over slow curves. The route was well marked with signs intelligently spaced and easy to follow. Snow began to fall as I drove through the hills and traffic compressed itself into a graceful procession.

I was remembering a tavern that loomed large in her history called The Stable. I had tried to describe to Lucy how she might be a figure dredged up from within. A delegate from dreamland. Not the most scientific theory I admit. Still it went some way toward explaining the absoluteness of my devotion. Lucy blinked at me over the rim of her wineglass not convinced.

Pair bonding, she said. Even molecules do it.

After the expressway I came upon a crowd milling under strings of high-powered light bulbs. A skating rink. I revved the motor at the edge of the ice and watched the gliding people colourful and plump in winter coats. They skated with passion hand in hand. Some were remarking as they went streaming by how their feet would be permanently ruined.

A girl waved to me as she passed nearly toppling herself in the process. In a moment she came round again and called out my name. Her breath turned to steam and the steam turned to ash.

# The Potential

Lover
You sank below the ground
When I was born
And from that moment on
Your muffled sobs have pounded in my ears
With every moan
Your ribcage rose and fell
Beneath my feet
And now my buried sister
You come creeping in my room
Combing grave dirt from your hair.
So alike
The buried alive
The walking dead
Such twins
As if reflection put on flesh and bone
Your face is my face
This body your own.
Many the mornings
On the fringe of sleep
I heard you singing
Dreamed of your return
No longer can a mirror keep
Our lips apart.

Before I wrap you hot and deathly pale
Within my arms
Pierce me    reach in
Compare hearts
Mine is the white one    lined
With theorems proofs and plots
Yours is the red pump
Pulsing with desire
So my long familiar twin
Let desire expire
In the heat of one embrace
From the far side of the eyelids
The inside of the face.

# All This Time

ALL THIS TIME, the car performed smoothly. So smoothly I forgot I was driving. It purred like some animal and I was its brain. A primitive brain on a Sunday drive.

I stopped at a cemetery and tried to work up hatred for Lucy by calling forth memories of broken promises and hasty words. I remembered the accusations the threats the lies and damnations. I remembered the strangers for whom her legs were always open. I remembered the clothes she was wearing the day she left town arm in arm with her former ex-fiancé. That was when I took up the mantle of the previous case.

Leaving the motor running I walked through the graveyard. Headstones tilted at crazy angles and despite the cold there was an odour of empty graves. The dead it seemed had departed. I saw in the light of a rising moon a thirty-foot crow speaking Hegel and Euclid. Subtle distinctions delicate equations issued from his great orange beak. His wings ruffled as he spoke of ideal matters and I sensed that the crow had found nothing to hate.

It was sweet to re-enter the car.

# Hermit

The choice was either solitude or murder
And it was mine
To live apart
Could the best friend fathom
Conversing over food and wine
The beast half-drooling to devour his heart?

A pretty face I knew a pretty face
And romance and its underneath
On whispered words I cut my teeth
But the taste for romance dulls
There is mercy in the synapse
Between two skulls

Racked by the pink of an imagined peach
A fasting man gets thinner by the dream
To me high noon brings images of men
Striding through a rainbow just beyond my reach
And then my quiet crumbles into prayer
In thanks that they are images not men

I know the score
I've huddled on this rock and slope
Nine years
Subtracting memory from hope
Let them sight me at the edge of town
I will be seen to be alone
Or what's a hermit good for?

# Tower

I BECAME A CAR in a hurry. An eastbound streak on Highway Five. Whizzing by the base of a huge tower I remembered Shelly, a pudgy girl who rented a room with a perfect view of it. She told me one night in a voice of fur and honey how she would stare at that tower as it went rosy in the twilight and simply yearn—implying lust for a quarter-mile of steel and concrete.

And there was Jack who planned to climb it lugging a spool of baling wire all the way to the top. He would wrap himself in the wire from head to foot and knot the last loop. Then measuring out the remaining wire to a length just twenty feet short of the distance to the ground he would secure the other end to the tower. He gave a cock-eyed grin and made a chopping motion with one hand: Sliced Jack.

The tower affected us all. For Lucy it was an occasion to seem wise, something she did well on occasion. I was slicing onions in the kitchen telling her about Jack. She appeared in the doorway with a calendar in one hand and a handful of silver in the other and held them out to me. Did she expect me to divide the time by the money?

No. She had to explain about Solomon.

# The Wisdom of Solomon

I prayed for thunder lightning
Or some other sign
That dreadful afternoon
But how exactly I remember
The blue arc of the sky
And how the sun blazed white
Upon the ivory throne

Surrounded by soldiers     pinned to fate
I knelt before my famous king
Too terrified to speak
While she stood beautiful with anger
Spitting out her lie
Solomon perused us with a lecher's eye
Son of David     king among kings

Let the child be cut in two!

A sword reared up at his command
I could not think
Or speak
Or stand

O Solomon     Solomon
There should have come a sign
Some angel bright with furious wing
For I am poor in speech and charms
But there are two of us who know
That woman and I know
Exactly what it was
You lowered squirming in her arms

# Off the Hook

THE CENTRE OF TOWN lay several miles to the south and by the time I reached King Street one of my shoes had sprung a leak. The snow was a dirty yellow veil under the streetlights. It softened the outlines of civilization.

Everything was closed.

I took shelter in one of the last remaining phone booths. My mind was off the hook. I put some coins on top of the phone and flipped through the torn bible of names. Lucy was still listed at the old address. The old number.

Snow and muddy glass, the downtown disappearing. On the far side of the moon a telephone was ringing and Lucy picked it up.

I yanked back the folding door and walked away. Behind me the receiver dangled by its silver cord squawking my name.

This happened not far from home.

# A Gold Chain

Just when I considered
Lucy was lying
Her lover sought me out
And explained everything
Nothing had happened really
It was autumn then
And I believed him
He offered me herbs
To take home and smoke
And bade me think on these things

When the smoke had cleared
She floated before me
With pearls around her throat
A fine gold chain about her hips
Just when I'd been certain
Lucy was faithful.

# Star

AS THE WIND TRAILED OFF and the night sky cleared I lay down on the grounds of the estate. Above me stars were set in a curve of sparkling logic. A dialectical tiara for the virgin world. The snow was deep and warm.

Disease delusion and a wealth of bad luck. That was the arrangement passing from the sky. Goodnight Lucy. I assigned a star to her where the sky rolled up with the horizon like a scroll.

# Dreams of Rescue

She dragged me from the river
My bloated carcass bitten and devoured

She washed me down
With healing potions
Singing softly bent above me
Words I couldn't understand
One foot in the river
One foot on the land.

Ah goddess of the rainbow
Angel of the sword
Of the precious things I've broken
What may be restored?
If what I did should be undone
Will I be cured? Or even thrive?
Will I grow pink
With satisfaction in the sun?

Bitten yes devoured by little things
A little man despising little things
Who sip by sip drains every dream and plan
A man afraid of sleep
Dreaming he's a man

# The Moon

SOMEONE HAD FASTENED the moon to an oak. It hung from a branch and lit a circle under the tree. I lay and listened to muffled words like hoof beats in my ears: what to bury. Whom to kiss.

The house was moored outside the patch of light windows blazing. I struggled to pin my attention on the moon. The night grew big with the instructions of that female voice: what to cling to. Whom to keep. It told me what to offer. What to grasp.

The voice was like the gypsy's voice I'd heard so long ago. She showed up at the door offering to tell me everything. I showed her Lucy's picture. A sample of her handwriting. A palm print. I even produced a lock of Lucy's hair. The gypsy examined them and muttered darkly. She pulled a pack of cards from her sleeve and spread them on the table.

The Moon turned up in Obstacles.

It was not the identical voice I was hearing now but the tone was much the same. What man shall die, what girl be free? Whom to love, to what degree.

# This Crosses Her

This for you
Shuffling down the street alone
In a raincoat and a pair of battered shoes

This for you
Drawn toward the beaten moon
Unsteadily as if the shoes are not your own

This for you
Shuffling down a street
Alone

# Death Warmed Over

BY NOW THE CAR and I were one. We made our re-entry following a zigzag route through the suburbs. The lawns and driveways were empty at this hour but there was an incident at a crossroads.

A woman and child were standing near a stop sign hand in hand. Their coats were too thin for the season and I could see as we drew near that they were shivering. Catching sight of us the woman clutched the child to her and spun away as if I were Death on a pale horse.

I got out of the car. The woman whimpered and backed away pressing the child's face to her chest. Her terror was so plain I reached out to reassure her. She screamed.

What would calm her? I began to tell her about R. a friend who had died while I was out of town. Died when I was on some dubious mission. The day after the funeral I received an email from him.

Snow began to fall and settle over mother and child and me. The story of R. turned to steam. Afterwards I watched the woman and child scuttle up the road and turn toward the centre of town. I looked at the car. It looked so hopeful. So long-suffering crouched in the falling snow.

But I knew it was over between us.

# An Email from R.

You told me you could write a song
Too holy to be sung
Too final for the audience
You found yourself among
But dying was the last thing
You hoped to master young
So you practised the art of illusion

Some who were not worthy
Saw you dressed up like a clown
Sweeping up the moonlight
From the jagged edge of town
You climbed out on the rooftop
No one could bring you down
And no one rushed up there to join you

You complained in your last postcard
How the moon refused to shine
On the self-inflicted torture
You were learning to refine
Your footprints wound in circles
High above the timberline
People claimed you were lost to begin with

Must I forgive the nurses
On whom I must depend?
They tell me if I sleep
A choir of doctors will descend
Well I don't plan to sleep that much
I don't expect to mend
And you're just a ghost to me lately

The night they came to get me
I remembered what you said
About a man composing nocturnes
For the sick and the dead
One by one the muses come
And nail him into bed
While you take a stroll in some forest

# Home

THE VOICE WHISPERED near my elbow as I crept to the dining-room window and peered inside. Scene of great conflict over which the ghosts yet lingered: when to lie down     with whom     to what end. It was in this room Lucy told me about her ex-fiancé (as he then was) in appalling detail. Voice fluttering in my ear: how to aim and whom to hunt. When to cry. On whose breast. For how long.

Next window. Feet numb with cold. A small bedroom also empty. The bed a battered raft floating in the middle. Icebound whispers and a violent sea. How to kneel     in what chapel     at what hour of day or night     whose cunt what bridge     to whose delight. Could one look at this room and speak of delight?

Sound of a car pulling up. I ducked into the hedge. The car switched off but no sound of closing door or moving feet—no sound except that fucking voice: whom to condemn     on what scale. Little cedars weighed down with snow. Far off on the highway headlights roamed: what river to fish     whose eyes to adore     in what parade whose pawn to take     when to yield.

It was my car.

# Horseman

Wednesday morning I saw the boy
He rode upon a stallion down a thin dirt road
Where hedges line the farmers' fields

The villagers turned out to watch him leave
Or peered through fences     curtains
Through gaps in green
White horse     naked child
Even the sunflowers turned
Toward his face.

But stranger still
They knew the stallion to be wild
Had seen how strong men broke their backs
Young wives who nursed them bleeding in the dirt
Crying out the nature of the beast
No man could tame or kill
And yet the boy just cantered out of town
Completely in control
Not innocent
The way he smiled.

A cynic muttered in his beard
Pretty infant rider fear the past
Your father's a dull clod
Your mother's vague soul
Evaporated Wednesday last

His fingers beaming down the generations
Shine on me
Years go by
Let the infant rider be my son
Let me die
At noon on Wednesday
He'll go riding like a legend from my side

# Remember Keep Holy

I HAVE CONSIDERED my people and will protect them all—Sliced Jack and Shelly. Lucy and the rest. And all of their friends and relations and theirs in turn and by extension their friends and relations also. Their loves have sewn my fingers to the wheel. How would it look if I were to let them perish at the crooking of my arm? The slightest lag in concentration and the world caves in to bury Jack for whom my friendship was imperfect to smother Shelly whom I did not care to kiss. To murder Lucy.

> Plant the field    then rest
> Name the child    then rest
> Wake up    release the bird    eat the meal
> Then rest    wash the cup    then rest,
> Wake up    take the pill    check the time
> Then rest
> Park the car    then rest
> Check the time    make the turn
> Fall asleep    then rest
> Fall asleep    then rest

Was it the car that kept me going?
From the voice a deep sigh. Your move.

# The Great Migration

This was the fifth season
above our heads infinity lay burning.

The multitude stretched north and south
along the shore. No breath of wind.
The Fool stood out amid the mortal ranks
of ones and zeroes     hair ash white
above the embers of his eyes

Small as children     hunched in dead
ill-fitting skins     the pale millions
shuffled through the sand toward the sea
No taste of salt
no feel of spray
tears without end
no breath of wind

Wheat for a penny?     a little one spoke
and shifted from foot to foot
Wheat for a penny? The Fool reached down
gave him nothing     wiped his tears away.

Fearful peace. Blasphemous calm sea.

The dead stepped into sleek black vessels
And rode them out to sea     arms upraised
toward the trumpet-coloured sky
Each one cast a silhouette
against a range of distant white-capped peaks.

Thus a thin girl to the Fool:
On love I was nourished for a time
and times     but half the time
to love was no sweeter than
failing to part
failing to part

      The Fool
reached out and wiped her tears away
then eased her coffin gently out to sea

# All That Was Mortal

ALL NIGHT I DREAMED of signposts the highway and its long slow curves. Music in the background. Many accidents. Many dead. The highway had been torn along the dotted line. Blood everywhere. Snow fluttered through moonlight and settled on bodies strewn along the roadside and women screaming. I drove on. Signs everywhere and the bloodied faces of women crying. And from the forest, voices.

Cancel my appointment

Hush     Drink deep.

Cancel my appointment

# Vanishing

Will no man pry a moral
Or some comfort from these seasons?
From my rooftop I can see
Wet snow falling
On islands     on waves
Where not a week ago
I watched the sailboats tack and turn
Day by day the seasons die     or change
Which is as good as death.

I close my eyes and see
The path I travelled
Not two nights ago
The lilies the roses
Damp at my feet
I see my planet trailing scarves
Of silk across the dark.
What bitterness
To kiss your lover as she vanishes.

From my rooftop I can see
The couples in the park
Driven only days ago
By lightning and a deadly sun
To flee the town's collapse.
Magician    empress    fool and priestess
Lie in pairs upon the green
Their brows are cool and glistening with dew
Their bodies slack    their eyes bruised
With nothing more than sleep
Amen. A second look:
At desperate islands in the wheeling snow
At fools who wake triumphant with a wink.